4 95

DATE DUE

NOV 2 0 198
NOV 1 9 198
JAN 2 3 195
MAR 1 1

D0760648

Zbigniew Herbert

SELECTED POEMS

*Translated with an Introduction
and Notes by*
John Carpenter and Bogdana Carpenter

OXFORD   LONDON   NEW YORK

OXFORD UNIVERSITY PRESS
1977

Oxford University Press, Walton Street, Oxford OX2 6DP

OXFORD LONDON GLASGOW NEW YORK
TORONTO MELBOURNE WELLINGTON CAPE TOWN
IBADAN NAIROBI DAR ES SALAAM LUSAKA
KUALA LUMPUR SINGAPORE JAKARTA HONG KONG TOKYO
DELHI BOMBAY CALCUTTA MADRAS KARACHI

British Library Cataloguing in Publication Data

Herbert, Zbigniew
    Selected poems of Zbigniew Herbert.
    I. Carpenter, John II. Carpenter, Bogdana
    891.8'5'17   PG7167.E64   77–30101
    ISBN 0–19–211861–7

*Printed in Great Britain by
The Bowering Press Ltd,
Plymouth.*

CONTENTS

PART TWO

INTRODUCTION

Zbigniew Herbert was born in Lvov in eastern Poland—now Russia—in 1924. He began to write poetry during the Second World War. In 1944 he studied at the Academy of Fine Arts, in Cracow, and a year later he entered the Academy of Commerce there; at this time he was a member of the literary club of *Logofagos*. In 1947 he received a Master's degree in economics and moved to Toruń, where he studied law at the Nicolas Copernicus University, and received the degree of Master of Laws in 1950. Herbert stayed on in Toruń to study philosophy, and was influenced by the philosopher Henryk Eizenberg—to whom he dedicated his poem 'To Marcus Aurelius'. In 1950 he lived briefly in Gdańsk where he worked for the *Merchant's Review*, before moving to Warsaw, where for the next six years he held a variety of jobs: in the Management Office of the Peat Industry, in the department for retired pensioners of the Teachers' Cooperative, as a part-time worker in a bank, in a store, and in the legal department of the Composers' Association.

His poems began to appear in periodicals in 1950, but none was published in book form until after the 'thaw' in 1956. Then his first two books were published almost simultaneously: *Chord of Light* in 1956, and in 1957 *Hermes, Dog, and Star*, which was twice as long as a normal volume of poems. Both of these books contained poems which he had been writing during the twelve preceding years. Other prominent poets of Herbert's generation, among them Miron Białoszewski and Tymoteusz Karpowicz, also had to wait out the Stalinist years before their work could be available to a wider public. The event of publication after years of enforced silence is poignantly described in Herbert's poem 'Drawer'.

His poetry received instant recognition and it seemed as if all of a sudden a major poet had appeared in full maturity and originality. But during the years after the war his poetry had steadily evolved; he had shown poems to friends, read them aloud, received criticism, and they had been copied; at this time most poets did not look to the publishing world for criticism. Herbert was influenced both by 'Catastrophists' such as Czesław Miłosz, who stressed philosophical and historical themes in their poetry, and by avant-garde poets of the nineteen-twenties and thirties such as Czechowicz who eschewed punctuation. Several other poets of Herbert's generation who lived through the war also turned to the avant-garde in their search for poetic forms which were capable of rendering their experience. Herbert was also influenced by two poets who died in the Warsaw Uprising of 1944, Tadeusz Gajcy and Krzysztof Baczyński.

The war—the Holocaust—was probably the most important experience in Herbert's life, and left an indelible imprint on his poetry. As late as 1969, in the poem 'Prologue' which introduced his fourth collection of poems, he wrote about those who took part in the war:

> I must carry them to a dry place
> and make a large mound of sand
> before spring strews flowers for them
> and a great green dream stupefies them.

The war permanently shaped his outlook. He was a young high school student when it broke out. The place where he was born and brought up became part of a foreign, totally inaccessible country. The face of Poland was permanently changed, socially, politically, and physically; the entire country was shifted several hundred miles to the west. These experiences partly explain Herbert's insistence on a clear moral stance which can resist the fluctuations of history and ideology. Another poet who lived through the war, Tadeusz Różewicz, has often been linked with Herbert, primarily because they are both of the same 'War

Generation' and because they are both moralists. But probably they should be contrasted, rather than associated with one another. Różewicz's poetry after the war emphasized purely personal experience and denied all previous values, whereas Herbert drew entirely different conclusions. He has written: 'Something makes me different from the "War Generation". It seems to me that I came away from the war without accepting the failure of the earlier morality. It is still attractive to me most of all because I painfully feel the lack of tablets of values in the contemporary world.'[1] Herbert's early poem 'Two Drops', which was written during the war, describes two lovers in a shelter during a bombardment; commenting on the poem Herbert says, 'It was unusual: in a situation like this, terror fills the whole person, forcing him to forget about those who are closest to him. The life instinct which is awoken in moments of total menace fills us ceaselessly with a rat's fear, with only the will to save oneself. And meanwhile these two people opposed to the raging cruelty the fragile power of love.'[2] Herbert is a more positive poet than most other members of the War Generation, although rarely have positive values been won against greater opposition and with greater struggle. 'History teaches us that nations and their achievements can be destroyed in an almost total manner. During the war I saw the fire of a library. The same fire was devouring wise and stupid books, good and bad. Then I understood that it is nihilism which menaces culture the most. Nihilism of fire, stupidity, and hatred.'[3]

A few words should be said about Herbert's use of the past. It is remarkably alive for him, and very much like the present; historical figures frequently appear in his poems. His version of the past might be described as an extension of the present, or a backwards continuation of it in which people are as alive as ourselves. In Western Europe a concern for the past is sometimes associated with reaction. In Poland during the decade

[1] Herbert, *Poezje wybrane*, Ludowa Spółdielnia Wydawnicza, Warszawa, 1970, p. 150.
[2] *Ibid.*, p. 7.
[3] *Ibid.*, p. 18.

after World War II, however, a paradoxical situation arose in which some of the writers who had most completely rejected the pre-war culture found they had little basis for rebelling against the Stalinist present; on the other hand, a poet like Herbert who strived to repossess the culture of the past was able to express revolt in one of its most intense and radical forms. For Herbert the past represented living experience rather than lifeless forms; he has written: 'I turn to history not for lessons in hope, but to confront my experience with the experience of others and to win for myself something which I should call universal compassion, but also a sense of responsibility, a sense of responsibility for the human conscience.'[4]

Herbert published his third volume of poetry, *Study of the Object*, in 1961. In the late nineteen-fifties he made his first trip to Western Europe. In 1962 his *Barbarian in the Garden* came out, a volume of essays on such topics as the construction of the Gothic cathedral, the paintings of Piero della Francesca, the cave paintings of Lascaux, and the ruins of Paestum. Herbert's prose style in this book is extremely interesting: it is an original combination of personal, richly poetic first-hand description, and highly analytical, scholarly research. Herbert spent the years 1965–71 abroad. For several years he was Poet-in-Residence at the Frei Universität in West Berlin, and he travelled to many countries, among them Greece, Italy, France, and the United States. He spent the year 1970–71 teaching at the City College of Los Angeles. While he was abroad his fourth volume of poems, *Inscription*, was published in Warsaw in 1969. A volume of plays, several of which had been written for the radio, was published in 1970. Herbert returned to Poland to live in 1971, and in that year his *Collected Poems* appeared, which contained most of the poems of his first four collections. In 1974 his fifth volume of poems, *Mr Cogito*, was published.

The present selection of Herbert's poems draws on all his work, but most heavily on the recent poems included in *Mr Cogito*. A few of the poems were written after that volume appeared, and these have been translated either from the

[4] Karl Dedecius, *Ein Gedicht und sein Autor*, Berlin, 1967, p. 156.

author's typescripts or from the periodical *Twórczość*. These poems, as well as those from *Mr Cogito*, comprise part II of this book, and all of them were written during the period 1969–1975. Part I draws from the earlier four books of poems, and with a single exception ('White Stone') the translations have been made from the texts in Herbert's *Collected Poems* (*Wiersze zebrane*, Czytelnik, Warszawa, 1971).[5]

One of the major principles of translation of these poems has been to *interpret* Herbert's meanings as thoroughly as possible. This is different from literalness; the translators have tried to recast Herbert's poems in English, using all the resources at their disposal. At the same time they have tried to resist any tendency to be reductive, to round off the texture or structure of a poem, or to adapt it to a particular audience, idiom, or expectation. This has meant the creation of a new speaking voice, a voice that can be heard, in English. This has not been easy; Herbert is a poet of distinctions as well as of powerful, expressive structures. The moralist's constant imperative, the *distinguo*, is present in highly compressed form in the smallest details of these poems. Herbert's stringent conscience also applies to his use of words, and the translators have tried to convey this rigorousness as well as the translation process permits.

At first glance, Herbert's poems appear easy to translate—they employ clear intellectual structures, and rhyme occurs rarely ('Drawer' and 'Prologue' are exceptions). On the other hand, Herbert's rhythms, tone, and word choice are often exceptionally difficult to translate, and his texture is complex. He uses a combination of high literary 'decorum'—or formality—with more intimate, conversational, and everyday speech to express his sense of truth, to conform to the contours of the world. The tension between these two styles or tones is always present, and they are always simultaneous. Often he follows the movement of thought—the special colloquialness of silent thinking—with the great agility typical of his style. In the poem

[5] The translators have tried to avoid duplicating poems which have already appeared in the Penguin edition of Herbert's *Selected Poems*, published in 1968.

an internal dialogue can occur between the poet and his conscience, or between the present and the past, which draws together associations from disparate sources into a tightly strung balance. Also, Herbert has a highly developed sense of metaphor. Metaphors frequently arise from a play on words. Contradictions are often present, as they must be when irony is used—and Herbert is a supreme ironist. A poem can be at the same time completely in earnest, and humorous. Sometimes Herbert uses the device of Mr Cogito, a tongue-in-cheek persona who often is clearly *not* to be believed in, to confront deeply personal problems and feelings. The translators have tried to give these seeming contradictions their due and to maintain them out of the firm conviction that they contribute to the larger emotional and intellectual meaning. English has special problems with its definite and indefinite articles (Polish has none), and a rather iron-clad word order which is incapable of producing many of the effects of the freer Polish word order. To surmount these problems, and others—each line requiring innumerable decisions—we have tried to enter into the Polish text as completely as possible. One of the translators is a native Polish speaker, the other a native English speaker; we have worked as a team, putting our resources together, and when we have been successful we have had an eerie sense of sympathy with the original texts, and with the author, akin to what Stanislavski described in his recommendations to the actor. A comparable sense of imaginative sympathy is described by Herbert at the end of his poem 'Sister'.

Some of these poems have first appeared in the following magazines: *The Times Literary Supplement, Poetry* (Chicago), *Books Abroad, Encounter, Modern Poetry in Translation, The Malahat Review, London Magazine, Europäische Hefte, Pacific Poetry* and *Fiction Review, Prism International, American Poetry Review,* and *Mr Cogito.*

Seattle, Washington, 1977   JOHN CARPENTER
BOGDANA CARPENTER

xiv

PART ONE

Island

There is a sudden island Sculpture of the sea cradle
graves between ether and salt
the smokes of its paths wind around rocks
and the raising of voices above drone and silence
Here seasons parts of the world have a home
and shadow is good good night and good sun
the ocean would be glad to leave its bones here
leaves bandage the tired shoulder of the sky
Its fragility among the screams of the elements
when at night human fire talks in the mountains
and at daybreak before dawn sparkles
first the light of the springs rises in the ferns.

Never About You

I never dare to speak about you
immense sky of my neighbourhood
nor about you roofs restraining the waterfall of the air
beautiful downy roofs hair of our homes
I am also silent about you chimneys laboratories of sadness
abandoned by the moon stretching your necks
and about you windows open—closed

I will not even describe the house
which knows all my escapes and returns
although it is small and doesn't leave my closed eyelid
nothing will render the smell of the green door-curtain
nor the creaking of the steps on which they bring a lit lamp
nor the leaf over the gate

I would really like to write about the knob of the gate of this
      house
about its rough clasp and friendly creak
and although I know so much about it
I repeat only a cruelly common litany of words

So many feelings are contained between one heartbeat and
      another
so many objects that can be grasped in both hands

Don't be surprised we don't know how to describe the world
and only speak to things affectionately by their first names

See

Blue cold as stone against which angels
haughty and very unearthly sharpen their wings
walking on rungs of glimmer and boulders of shadow
they sink slowly into the imaginary sky
but after a moment come out even paler
on the other side of the sky on the other side of the eyes
don't say it isn't true there are no angels
immersed in the pool of your lazy body
you who see everything with the colour of your eyes
and sated with the world you stop—
on the border of your eyelashes

White Stone

Only close the eyes—

my step walks away from me
like a deaf bell the air will absorb it
and a voice my own voice which calls from afar
freezes into a little puff of vapour
the hands drop
cupped around the calling mouth

touch a blind animal
will recede into depth
into dark and humid caves
the smell of the body will remain
wax burning

then grows in me
not fear not love
but white stone

so this is how the fate is fulfilled
which draws us on the mirror of a bas-relief
I see the concave face convex chest and hollow shells of knees
the feet upturned a bundle of dry toes

deeper than the blood of the earth
more luxuriant than a tree
is the white stone
indifferent fullness

but again the eyes shout
the stone recedes
again it is a grain of sand
sunk under the heart

we swallow images we are filling emptiness
the voice struggles with space
ears hands lips tremble under waterfalls
in the shell of the nostrils enters
a ship carrying aromas from India
and rainbows blossom from the sky to the eyes

wait white stone

only close the eyes

On Translating Poetry

Like an awkward bumble-bee
he sits on the flower
until the delicate stalk bends
he squeezes through rows of petals
like the pages of a dictionary
he tries to reach the centre
where the scent and sweetness are
and though he has a cold
and lacks any taste
still he perseveres
until he knocks his head
against the yellow pistil

and here already is the end
it is difficult to penetrate
from the cups of flowers
to their roots
so the bumble-bee goes out
very proud
and loudly buzzing:
I have been inside
and to those
who don't quite believe him
he shows his nose
yellow with pollen

Classic

A wooden ear, enormous, plugged with cotton and the tediousness of Cicero. What a great stylist, everyone says. To-day no one writes such long sentences. And what erudition. He even knows how to read inscriptions on stone. Only never will he guess that the marble veins in the Baths of Diocletian are the blood vessels of slaves which have burst in the quarries.

Seamstress

Since morning it rains. There will be the funeral of the one who lived opposite. Of the seamstress. She dreamed of a wedding ring, and died with a thimble on her finger. Everybody laughs at that. The kind-hearted rain darns the sky with earth. But nothing will come of that either.

Painter

Under walls white as a birch forest the ferns of paintings grow. In an odour of turpentine and oils Miron recreates the drama of a lemon condemned to coexistence with a green drapery. There is also a female nude.

—My fiancée, says Miron. She posed for me during the occupation. It was winter, without bread and coal. The blood gathered into small blue blots under her white skin. It was then that I painted the warm pink background.

Mad Woman

Her burning look holds me tightly in an embrace. She says words mixed with dreams. She invites. You will be happy if you come to believe and hitch your cart to a star. She is gentle when she nurses the clouds with her breasts, but when calm has left her she runs on the seashore and throws her arms into the sky.

In her eyes I see how two angels have come to stand at my shoulders: the pale, malicious angel of Irony, and the powerful, loving angel of Schizophrenia.

Fish

It is impossible to imagine the sleep of fish. Even in the darkest corner of the pond, among the reeds, their rest is vigilance: eternally the same position and absolute impossibility to say of them: they have rested their heads.

Also their tears are like a cry in a void —countless.

Fish cannot gesticulate their despair. This justifies the dull knife which jumps on the back and flays the sequins of the scales.

Conch

In front of the mirror in my parents' bedroom lay a pink conch. I used to approach it on tiptoes, and with a sudden movement put it against my ears. I wanted to surprise it one day when it wasn't longing with a monotonous hum for the sea. Although I was small I knew that even if we love someone very much, at times it happens that we forget about it.

Violins

Violins are naked. They have thin arms. Clumsily they try to protect themselves with them. They cry from shame and cold. That's why. And not, as the music critics maintain, so it will be more beautiful. This is not true.

Gauguin the End

With mango flowers in white weather and black rain
on the rue des Fourneaux and on the Pacific
huge Gauguin opens a wide path among paintings
and leaves with the heavy blunt noise of wooden shoes
he looks for a spring then drinks a long time
the sky opened with a knife and falls sweetly asleep

he didn't desire rest he desired sleep
which is a labour a long march at midday
with dark buckets of images

                              sometimes he still hears
the hiss of Parisian salons a white woman
remained at home he drew the curtain
she probably still sleeps
let her sleep

vomit of the ocean guitars parakeets
he didn't love girls neither Tehura
nor Metta Gad with a thread of saliva between her lips
Alina died too early he was repulsed by mould

a big cart is rolling with mango flowers
the last king Pomare a rotting pineapple
goes to the earth with the uniform of an admiral
a wooden bell is ringing

patient Vincent is in sun like a sunflower
the sun burns through the brownish-red brain
he had courage and painted with a razor
he is not Monet who shouted I won't exhibit
avec le premier barbouilleur venu

he who understood cobalt had to leave the stock exchange
there was no other road only the road to the sea
on his elbows and knees Gauguin drives his body
fruits are like abcesses forests like lichens
Maori gods poke intently in their teeth
vomit of the ocean guitars parakeets

between the sky of fire and grass of fire—snow
a Breton hamlet in mango flowers

Dawn

The first voice resounds in the deepest
moment before dawn, blunt and sharp at
the same time, like the blow of a knife.
Then from minute to minute the rising
murmurs drill through the trunk of night.

It seems there is no hope.

That which struggles for light is mortally fragile.

And when on the horizon appears the
cross-section of a tree, stained with
blood, unreally large and truly painful,
do not forget to bless the miracle.

Path

It wasn't a path of truth but simply a path
with a brown root across needles on the sides
the forest was full of berries and unreliable spirits

it wasn't a path of truth because suddenly
it lost its unity and from then on in life
our goals were unclear

                    To the right was a spring

if you chose the spring you went through steps of half-light
touch led blindly into deeper and deeper darkness
to the mother of elements honoured by Thales
in order to unite finally with the humid heart of things
with the dark grain of cause

                    To the left was a hill

it gave calm and a sweeping view
the border of the forest its dark mass
without individual leaves trunks wild strawberries
without the soothing knowledge the forest is one of many
        forests

Is it truly impossible to have at the same time
the source and the hill the idea and the leaf
and to pour multiplicity without devils' ovens
of dark alchemy of too clear an abstraction

13

On the Road to Delphi

It was on the road to Delphi. I had just passed a red rock when from the opposite side Apollo appeared. He walked rapidly, without paying attention to anything. As he approached I noticed that he was playing with the Medusa's head, shrivelled and dried from age. He was whispering something under his breath. If I heard correctly, he was repeating: 'A craftsman must probe to the very bottom of cruelty.'

Hermes, Dog, and Star

Hermes goes through the world. He meets a dog.

—I am a god, Hermes introduces himself politely.

The dog sniffs his feet.

—I feel lonely. Humans betray gods; but unknowing, mortal animals, we crave them. In the evening, after a whole day wandering, we will sit down under an oak. I will tell you then that I feel old and want to die. It will be a necessary lie, so you will lick my hands.

—All right, the dog carelessly replies, I will lick your hands. They are cool, and have a strange smell.

They walk, they walk. They meet a star.

—I am Hermes, the god says, and produces one of his very best faces. Would you like to go with us to the end of the world? I will make it frightening there, so you will have to lean your head on my shoulder.

—Good, the star replies with a glassy voice. It's all the same to me where I go; but the end of the world, that is naïve. Unfortunately there is no end of the world.

They go. They go. The dog, Hermes, and the star. They hold hands. Hermes thinks that if he sets out to find friends another time, he won't be so frank.

The Sacrifice of Iphigenia

Agamemnon is closest to the pyre. He has thrown a coat over his head, but hasn't closed his eyes. He thinks that through the fabric he will perceive the glimmer which melts his daughter like a hairpin.

Hippias stands in the front row of soldiers. He sees only the small mouth of Iphigenia which breaks with weeping, as it did when they had a terrible quarrel because she pinned flowers in her hair and let unknown men accost her on the street. Again and again the vision of Hippias grows immeasurably longer, and the small mouth of Iphigenia occupies the huge space from the sky to the earth.

Calchas, his eyes glazed with leucoma, sees everything in the hazy insect-like light. The only thing that really moves him is the drooping sails of the ships in the bay, which at this moment make the sadness of old age seem unbearable to him. Therefore he lifts his hand for the sacrifice to begin.

The chorus placed on the hillside takes in the world with its correct proportions. The small shining bush of the pyre, white priests, purple kings, loud copper and the miniature fires of soldiers' helmets, all this against a background of bright sand and the immense colour of the sea.

The view is superb, with the help of the proper perspective.

The Missing Knot

Clytemnestra opens the window, looks at herself in the glass to put on her new hat. Agamemnon stands in the vestibule, lights a cigarette, and waits for his wife. Aegisthus comes in at the main door. He doesn't know that Agamemnon returned home last night. They meet on the stairs. Clytemnestra suggests that they go to the theatre. From now on they will be going out a lot together.

Electra works in the cooperative. Orestes studies pharmacology. Soon he'll marry his careless classmate with the pale complexion and eyes continually filled with tears.

Ornamental yet True

Three-dimensional illustrations from deplorable textbooks. Deathly white with dry hair, an empty quiver, and a wilted thyrsus. They stand immobile on barren islands, among the living stones, under a leafy sky. Symmetrical Aphrodite, Jove mourned by his dogs, Bacchus drunk with plaster. A disgrace to nature. The lichen of the gardens.

The real gods entered the skin of stones only for a short time and unwillingly. The immense enterprise—of thunder and dawns, hunger and golden rains—required unusual mobility. They ran from burning cities, they sailed to distant islands clinging to a wave. In beggars' rags they crossed the frontiers of ages and civilizations.

Hunting and hunted, sweating, noisy, in the unending pursuit of fleeing humanity.

Attempt to Dissolve Mythology

The gods met in a shack at the outskirts of town. Zeus as usual made a long and boring speech. The ultimate conclusion: we must dissolve the organization, enough senseless conspiracy, we must enter this rational society and somehow survive. Athena was whimpering in the corner.

The final profits were divided honestly—this should be stressed. Poseidon had an optimistic attitude; he roared loudly that he'll manage all right. The guardians of navigable streams and cleared forests felt the worst. Privately they all counted on dreams, but no one wanted to speak about them.

No motions were passed. Hermes abstained from voting. Athena whimpered in the corner.

Late in the evening they were returning to the city with forged papers in their pockets and handfuls of small change. As they crossed a bridge Hermes jumped into the river. They watched him drown, but no one tried to save him.

Opinions were divided as to whether this was a bad omen or, on the contrary, a good one. At any rate it was a starting point toward something new and uncertain.

Apollo and Marsyas

The real duel of Apollo
with Marsyas
(perfect ear
versus immense range)
is held at dusk
when as we already know
the judges
have awarded victory to the god

tightly bound to a tree
meticulously flayed of his skin
Marsyas
shouts
before the shout reaches
his tall ears
he rests in the shadow of that shout

shuddering with disgust
Apollo is cleaning his instrument

only apparently
is the voice of Marsyas
monotonous
and composed of a single vowel
A

in reality
Marsyas
tells
of the inexhaustible wealth
of his body

bald mountains of liver
white ravines of aliment
rustling forests of lung
sweet hills of muscle
joints bile blood and shudders
the wintry wind of bone
over the salt of memory

shuddering with disgust
Apollo is cleaning his instrument

now to the chorus
is joined the backbone of Marsyas
in principle the same A
only deeper with the addition of rust

this is beyond the endurance
of the god with nerves of plastic

> along a gravel path
> hedged with box-trees
> the victor departs
> wondering
> whether out of Marsyas' howling
> will not one day arise
> a new kind
> of art—let us say—concrete

suddenly
at his feet falls
a petrified nightingale

he turns his head
and sees
that the tree to which Marsyas was tied
is white

completely

Shore

It waits at the shore of a large and slow river
on the other side is Charon the sky shines turbidly
(besides it is not sky at all) Charon
is already here he only throws a rope around a branch
it (the soul) takes out the obol
which isn't sour yet under the tongue
it sits in the back of the empty boat
all this without a word

if there were at least the moon
or the howling of a dog

Prologue

He
For whom do I play? For the closed window
for the door-handle shining arrogantly
for the bassoon of rain—for the sad rain-pipe
for the rats dancing among the dead

The last drum was bombs
in the courtyard there was a simple funeral
two planks in a cross and a helmet full of holes
in the sky a great rose of fires

Chorus
The calf turns on the spit.
In the oven the brown bread ripens.
Fires die out. Only the flame which is contained lasts forever.

He
And the coarse inscription on those planks
short names like a volley
'Gryf' 'Wilk' and 'Pocisk' who remembers
faded in rain the colour of ore

For long years afterwards we laundered
the bandages   Now no one cries
the buttons from a soldier's coat
rattle in a matchbox

Chorus ·
Throw away memories. Burn remembrance and enter the stream
    of a new life.
There is only earth. One earth and the seasons of the year are
    over it.
Wars of insects—wars of people and short death on the flower
    of honey.
The grain ripens. The oaks flourish. Rivers go from mountains
    to the ocean.

He
I flow upstream and they with me
they look in the eye implacably
they stubbornly whisper old words
we eat our bitter bread of despair

I must carry them to a dry place
and make a large mound of sand
before spring strews flowers for them
and a great green dream stupefies them

This city—

Chorus
There is no such city
It has gone under the earth

21

He
It still shines

Chorus
Like rotten wood in the forest

He
An empty place
but the air above it continually trembles
after those voices

                    *   *   *

The ditch where a muddy river flows
I call the Vistula. It is hard to confess:
they have sentenced us to such love
they have pierced us through with such a fatherland

The Rain

When my older brother
came back from the war
he had a little silver star on his forehead
and under the star
an abyss

a splinter of shrapnel
hit him at Verdun
or perhaps at Grünwald
(he didn't remember the details)

22

he talked a lot
in many languages
but most of all he liked
the language of history

until losing breath
he called to his dead comrades under the ground
Roland Jones Hannibal

he shouted
that this is the last crusade
soon Carthage will fall
and then sobbing confessed
that Napoleon doesn't like him

we watched
him become paler
his senses abandoned him
slowly he was turning into a monument

into musical shells of ears
entered a stone forest

the skin of his face
was fastened
with two blind dry
buttons of eyes

all he had left
was touch

what stories
he told with his hands
in the right he had romances
in the left soldier's memories

they took my brother
and carried him out of town

he returns now every autumn
thin and quiet
he doesn't want to enter the house
he knocks at the window for me to come out

we walk on the streets
and he tells me
unbelievable tales
touching my face
with blind fingers of weeping

Warsaw Cemetery

This wall
of the last view
is not here

lime for houses and graves
lime for memory

the last echo of a salvo
formed into a stone slab
and a terse inscription
engraved in peaceful Roman script

> the dead flee the invasion of the living
> they descend more deeply
> lower down

24

they complain at night in the pipes of sorrow
they come out cautiously
drop by drop

once again they flare up
with the simple scratch of a match

and on the surface calm
slabs lime for memory

on the corner of an avenue of the living
and the new world
under the proudly knocking heel
gathers like a molehill
the cemetery of those who ask
for a mound of loose earth
for a faint sign from above the surface

Biology Teacher

I can't remember
his face

he stood high above me
on long spread legs
I saw
the little gold chain
the ash-grey frock coat
and the thin neck
on which was pinned
a dead necktie

he was the first to show us
the leg of a dead frog
which touched by a needle
violently contracts

he led us
through a golden microscope
to the intimate life
of our great-grandfather
the slipper animalcule

he brought
a dark kernel
and said: claviceps

encouraged by him
I became a father
at the age of ten
when after tense anticipation
a yellow sprout appeared
from a chestnut submerged in water
and everything broke into song
all around

in the second year of the war
the rascals of history
killed the teacher of biology

if he reached heaven—

perhaps he is walking now
on the long rays
dressed in grey stockings
with a huge net
and a green box
gaily swinging on his back

but if he didn't go up there—

when on a forest path
I meet a beetle scrambling
up a hill of sand
I come close to him
click my heels
and say:
—Good morning professor
would you let me help you

I lift him over carefully
and for a long time look after him
until he disappears
in the dark faculty room
at the end of the corridor of leaves

The Substance

Neither in heads snuffed out by the piercing shadow of pennons
nor in open breasts left on a field of stubble
neither in hands bearing the cold sceptre and orb
nor in the heart of a bell
nor under the feet of a cathedral
in the sum of everything

those who draw their carts through badly paved suburbs
and flee from fires with a bottle of borsch
who return to the ruins not to claim the dead
but to recover the pipe of an iron stove
starved—loving life
beaten on the face—loving life

27

whom it is difficult to call flowers
but who are flesh
that is living plasma
two hands for covering the head
two feet quick in retreat
the ability to gather food
the ability to breathe
the ability to transmit life under a prison wall
those perish
who love beautiful words more than fat smells
fortunately they are few

the nation endures
and returning with full sacks from its routes of retreat
builds triumphant arches
for the beautiful dead

To the Hungarians

We stand at the border
we stretch out our hands
and an immense rope made out of air
we bind brothers for you

from a broken shout
from clenched fists
a bell is moulded and the heart
silently they announce terror

the wounded stones beseech
the dead water beseeches
we stand at the border
we stand at the border

we stand at the border
called reason
and we look into the fire
and admire death

1956

The Wall

We are standing under the wall. Our
youth has been taken off like a shirt from
the condemned men. We wait. Before the
fat bullet will sit down on the nape of the
neck, ten, twenty years pass. The wall is
high and strong. Behind the wall is a tree
and a star. The tree pries at the wall with
its roots. The star nibbles the stone like a
mouse. In a hundred, two hundred years
there will already be a small window.

'It is fresh . . .'

it is fresh
as if today's
with thick blood on the surface
large as a deep-sea fish

he is carrying it around the city squares
he sprinkles it with salt
praises it with a loud voice

it is fresh
as if today's
these purple veins
don't prove anything really

they come near
they feel it with their fingers
shake their heads

when he hides it on his chest
then he truly feels
how fresh it is
still warm

it is fresh
as if today's
shamelessly large

who will take the wound

Episode from Saint-Benoît

In an old abbey on the Loire
(all sap from the trees flowed down this river)
in front of the entrance to the basilica
(not the narthex but a stone allegory)
on one of the capitols
stands the naked Max Jacob
over whom Satan and a four-winged archangel
are fighting

the result of the contest
has not been announced
unless you take into consideration
a neighbouring capitol

Satan firmly holds
the torn-off hand of Jacob
permitting the rest
to bleed itself away
among the archangel's four invisible wings

Drawer

O my seven-stringed board
here my dried tears were stored
my rebel's fist stiff in dissent
and paper where one cold night I wrote
my ridiculous youthful testament

now it's swept out empty
I sold the tears and the bunch of fists
at the market place they had a price
a little fame a few pennies
now no frightened sleep for me
and now no more concrete and lice

o drawer lost lyre
I still could play so much
drumming with my fingers on your empty floor
and how good was a desperate heart
therefore how difficult it is to part
from nourishing pain without hope

I knock on you forgive me open
I could be silent no longer
I had to sell the mark of my rebellion
such is freedom one has again
to invent and overthrow gods when
already Caesar wrestles with song

and now the empty seashell
hums about seas which sank into sand
about the storm shrunk to a salt crystal
before a drawer receives the body
such is my awkward prayer
to the four boards of morality

PART TWO

Mother

He fell from her knees like a ball of yarn.
He unwound in a hurry and ran blindly away.
She held the beginning of life. She would wind it
on her finger like a ring, she wanted to preserve him.
He was rolling down steep slopes, sometimes
he was climbing up. He would come back tangled, and be silent.
Never will he return to the sweet throne of her knees.

The stretched-out hands are alight in the darkness
like an old town.

Remembering my Father

His face severe in clouds above the waters of childhood
so rarely did he hold my warm head in his hands
given to belief not forgiving faults
because he cleared out woods and straightened paths
he carried the lantern high when we entered the night

I thought I would sit at his right hand
and we would separate light from darkness
and judge those of us who live
—it happened otherwise

a junk-dealer carried his throne on a hand-cart
and the deed of ownership the map of our kingdom

he was born for a second time slight very fragile
with transparent skin hardly perceptible cartilage
he diminished his body so I might receive it

D   35

in an unimportant place there is shadow under a stone

he himself grows in me we eat our defeats
we burst out laughing
when they say how little is needed
to be reconciled

Sister

Thanks to a slight difference in age to childish intimacy
a common bath the mystery of fluffy hair and soft skin
the small Cogito discovered—he could be his sister
(it was as simple as changing places at table
when the parents were out and grandmother permitted every-
     thing)
and she the owner of his name his bow his man's bicycle well
     even his nose
luckily they had different noses the lack of physical resemblance
let them avoid dramatic consequences
it ended with touch touch didn't open
and the young Cogito remained in the limits of his own skin

a grain of doubt the undermining of the *principium*
     individuationis
was deeply implanted however and one afternoon
the thirteen-year-old Cogito saw on the Street of the Legions
a horse cabman
he felt he was him so completely
that a red moustache broke out
and the cold whip burned his hand

Sense of Identity

If he had a sense of identity it was probably with a stone
with sandstone not too crumbly light light-grey
which has a thousand eyes of flint
(a senseless comparison the stone sees with its skin)
if he had a feeling of profound union it was exactly with a stone

it wasn't at all the idea of invariability the stone
was changeable lazy in the sunshine brightened like the moon
at the approach of a storm it became dark slate like a cloud
then greedily drank the rain and this wrestling with water
sweet annihilation the struggle of forces clash of elements
the loss of one's own nature drunken stability
were both beautiful and humiliating

so at last it would become sober in the air dried by thunder
embarrassing sweat the passing mist of erotic fervours

Mr Cogito Meditates on Suffering

All attempts to remove
the so-called cup of bitterness—
by reflection
frenzied actions on behalf of homeless cats
deep breathing
religion—
failed

one must consent
gently bend the head
not wring the hands
make use of the suffering gently moderately
like an artificial limb
without false shame
but also without unnecessary pride

do not brandish the stump
over the heads of others
don't knock with the white cane
against the windows of the well-fed

drink the essence of bitter herbs
but not to the dregs
leave carefully
a few sips for the future

accept
but simultaneously
isolate within yourself
and if it is possible
create from the matter of suffering
a thing or a person

play
with it
of course
play

entertain it
very cautiously
like a sick child
forcing at last
with silly tricks
a faint
smile

Mr Cogito Reads the Newspaper

On the first page
a report of the killing of 120 soldiers

the war lasted a long time
you could get used to it

      close alongside
      the news of a sensational crime
      with a portrait of the murderer

      the eye of Mr Cogito
      slips indifferently
      over the soldiers' hecatomb
      to plunge with delight
      into the description of everyday horror

a thirty-year-old farm labourer
under the stress of nervous depression
killed his wife
and two small children

it is described with precision
the course of the murder
the position of the bodies
and other details

for 120 dead
you search on a map in vain

too great a distance
covers them like a jungle

they don't speak to the imagination
there are too many of them
the numeral zero at the end
changes them into an abstraction

a subject for meditation:
the arithmetic of compassion

To Take Objects Out

To take objects out of their royal silence one must use either a stratagem or a crime. The frozen lake of a door is broken by the knocking of a carouser, a goblet dropped on the parquet floor gives an abrupt shriek like a glass bird, and a house which has been set on fire talks with the loquacious language of flames, with the language of a breathless epic poet, about what the bed, the chests, and the curtain were silent.

Mr Cogito and the Movement of Thoughts

Thoughts cross the mind
says the popular expression

the popular expression
overestimates the movement of thoughts

most of them
stand motionless
in the middle of a dull landscape
of ashy hills
parched trees

sometimes they come
to the bursting river of another's thoughts
they stand on the shore
on one leg
like hungry herons

with sadness
they remember the dried-up springs

they turn in a circle
searching for grain

they don't cross
because they will never arrive
they don't cross
because there is nowhere to go

they sit on stones
wring their hands
under the cloudy
low
sky
of the skull

Mr Cogito's Alienations

Mr Cogito holds in his arms
the warm amphora of a head

the rest of the body is hidden
only touch sees it

he looks at the sleeping head
strange yet full of tenderness

once again
he notices with amazement
that someone exists outside of him
impenetrable
like a stone

with limits
which open
only for a moment
then the sea casts it up
on the rocky shore

with its own blood
strange sleep
armed with its own skin

Mr Cogito removes
the sleeping head
gently

not to leave
on the cheek
the imprints of fingers

and he goes away
alone
into the lime of the sheets

43

Houses of the Outskirts

On a sunless autumn afternoon Mr Cogito likes
to visit the dirty outskirts of the city. There
is no purer source of melancholy, he says.

Houses of the outskirts with black-ringed windows
houses coughing quietly
shivers of plaster
houses with thin hair
sick complexion

only the chimneys dream
the lean complaint
reaches the edge of the forest
a shore of vast water

       I would like to invent names for you
       to fill you with the scent of India
       the fire of the Bosporus
       murmur of waterfalls

houses of the outskirts with sunken temples
houses chewing breadcrusts
cold as the sleep of a paralytic
whose stairways are palmtrees of dust
houses always for sale
inns of misfortune
houses which were never at the theatre

       the rats of the houses of the outskirts
       lead them to the shore of the ocean
       let them sit in the hot sand
       let them watch the tropical night
       let the wave reward them with a stormy ovation
       as befits only wasted lives

Sequoia

Gothic towers of needles in the valley of a stream
not far from Mount Tamalpais where in the morning and
evening thick fog comes like the wrath and passion of the ocean

in this reservation of giants they display a cross-section of a tree
     the coppery stump of the West
with immense regular veins like rings on water
and someone perverse has inscribed the dates of human history
an inch from the middle of the stump the fire of distant Rome
     under Nero
in the middle the battle of Hastings the night expedition of the
     drakkars
panic of the Anglo-Saxons the death of the unfortunate Harold
it is told with a compass
and finally right next to the beach of the bark the landing of the
     Allies in Normandy

the Tacitus of this tree was a geometrician and he did not know
     adjectives
he did not know syntax expressing terror he did not know any
     words
therefore he counted added years and centuries as if to say there
     is nothing
beyond birth and death nothing only birth and death
and inside the bloody pulp of the sequoia

Mr Cogito Considers the Difference between the Human Voice and the Voice of Nature

The oration of the worlds is untiring

I can repeat all of it from the beginning
with a pen inherited from a goose and Homer
with a diminished spear
stand in front of the elements

I can repeat all of it from the beginning
the hand will lose to the mountain
the throat is weaker than a spring
I will not outshout the sand
not with saliva tie a metaphor
the eye with a star
and with the ear next to a stone
I won't bring out stillness
from the grainy silence

and yet I gathered so many words in one line—longer than all
the lines of my palm and therefore longer than fate in a line
aiming beyond in a line blossoming in a luminous line in a line
which is to save me in the column of my life—straight as cour-
age a line strong as love—but it was hardly a miniature of the
horizon

and the thunderbolts of flowers continue to roll on the oration
    of grass the oration of clouds
choruses of trees mutter rock blazes quietly
the ocean extinguishes the sunset the day swallows the night
    and on the pass of the winds
new light rises

and morning mist lifts the shield of islands

History of the Minotaur

The true history of the prince Minotaur is told in the script Linear A, which has not yet been deciphered. Notwithstanding later gossip he was the authentic son of King Minos and Pasiphaë. The boy was born healthy, but with an abnormally large head which the fortune-tellers interpreted as a sign of future wisdom. In reality, with the years the Minotaur grew into a strong and somewhat melancholy—nitwit. The king decided to turn him over to the priesthood. But the priests explained that they could not admit the abnormal prince because it would lower the authority of religion, which had already been damaged by the invention of the wheel.

Consequently, Minos brought over an engineer then fashionable in Greece, Daedalus—creator of a noted branch of pedagogical architecture. This is how the labyrinth was built. By a system of corridors, from the simplest to the more complicated, by a difference in levels and a staircase of abstractions it was supposed to initiate the prince Minotaur into the principles of correct thinking.

So the miserable prince mooned about in the corridors of induction and deduction, pushed by his preceptors; he looked at the instructive frescoes with a vacant stare. He didn't understand a thing.

When King Minos had exhausted all his resources he decided to get rid of the disgrace to the family. He brought over (also from Greece, which was famous for capable people) the skilful murderer Theseus. And Theseus killed the Minotaur. On this point, myth and history are in agreement.

Through the labyrinth—by now an unnecessary school primer —Theseus returns carrying the huge, blood-stained head of the Minotaur, its eyes bulging, where for the first time wisdom began to sprout—which usually is brought by experience.

Damastes (Also Known as Procrustes) Speaks

My movable empire between Athens and Megara
where I ruled alone over forests ravines precipices
without a sceptre with a simple club without the advice of old
    men
dressed only in the shadow of a wolf

nor did I have subjects
if I had subjects they did not live as long as dawn

experts on mythology are mistaken who call me a bandit
in reality I was a scholar and social reformer
my real passion was anthropometry

I constructed a bed with the measurements of a perfect man
I compared the travellers I caught with this bed
I couldn't avoid—I admit—stretching limbs cutting legs

the patients died but the more there were who perished
the more I was certain my research was right
since what kind of progress is without victims

I longed to abolish the difference between the high and the low
I wanted to give to disgustingly varied humanity a single form
I did everything to make people equal

my head was cut off by Theseus the murderer of the innocent
    Minotaur
the one who used a woman's ball of yarn to escape from the
    labyrinth
a clever one without principles or vision of the future

I have a well-grounded hope that others will continue my labour
and bring the task so wonderfully begun to its end

Anabasis

The condottieri of Cyrus a foreign legion
cunning pitiless if necessary they killed
two hundred and fifteen daily marches
'kill us we can't go any further'
thirty-four thousand two hundred and fifty-five stadia

festering with sleeplessness they went through uncertain
     fords
mountain passes in snow salty plateaus
cutting a road in the living body of peoples
luckily they didn't lie they were defending civilization

the famous shout on Mount Teches
is mistakenly interpreted by melodiously coughing poets
they simply found the sea that is the exit from the dungeon

they made the journey without the Bible without prophets
     without burning bushes
without signs on the earth without signs in the sky
with the cruel consciousness that life is great

Caligula

*Reading old chronicles poems and lives Mr Cogito
sometimes experiences the physical presence of persons
long dead*

CALIGULA SPEAKS:

of all the citizens of Rome
I loved only one
Incitatus—the horse

when he entered the senate
the spotless toga of his coat
glistened immaculately among the purple-trimmed
      cowardly murderers

Incitatus was full of qualities
he never gave speeches
a stoic nature
I think he read the philosophers in the stable at night

I loved him so much one day I decided to crucify him
but his noble anatomy resisted it

he accepted the rank of consul indifferently
he performed his duties excellently
that is he didn't perform them at all

it was impossible to incite him to a lasting bond of love
with my second wife Caesonia
thus unfortunately a line of Caesar-Centaurs did not come
      into being

this is why Rome fell

I decided to appoint him a god
but on the ninth day before the calends of February
Cherea Cornelius Sabinus and other fools hindered these
      pious intentions

calmly he accepted the news of my death

he was thrown out of the palace and condemned to exile

he bore this blow with dignity

he died without progeny
slaughtered by a thick-skinned butcher from the locality of
      Ancium

about the posthumous fate of his meat
Tacitus is silent

Mr Cogito Tells about the Temptation of Spinoza

Baruch Spinoza of Amsterdam
was seized by a desire to reach God

in the attic
cutting lenses
he suddenly pierced a curtain
and stood face to face

he spoke for a long time
(and as he so spoke
his mind enlarged
and his soul)
he posed questions
about the nature of man

—distracted God stroked his beard

—he asked about the first cause

—God looked into infinity

—he asked about the final cause

—God cracked his knuckles
cleared his throat

when Spinoza became silent
God spake

—you talk nicely Baruch
I like your geometric Latin
and the clear syntax
the symmetry of your arguments

let's speak however
about Things Truly
Great

—look at your hands
cut and trembling

—you destroy your eyes
in the darkness

—you are badly nourished
you dress shabbily

—buy a new house
forgive the Venetian mirrors
that they repeat surfaces

—forgive flowers in the hair
the drunken song

—look after your income
like your colleague Descartes

—be cunning
like Erasmus

—dedicate a treatise
to Louis XIV
he won't read it anyway

—calm
the rational fury
thrones will fall because of it
and stars turn black

52

—think
about the woman
who will give you a child

—you see Baruch
we are speaking about Great Things

—I want to be loved
by the uneducated and the violent
they are the only ones
who really hunger for me

now the curtain falls
Spinoza remains alone

he does not see the golden cloud
the light on the heights

he sees darkness

he hears the creaking of the stairs
footsteps going down

Georg Heym—the Almost Metaphysical Adventure

If it is true
an image precedes thought
one would believe
that the ideas of Heym
originated while ice skating

—the ease of moving
over the icy surface

he was there and here
he circled around the moving centre
he wasn't a planet
nor a bell
nor a farmer tied to his plough

—the relativity of movement
mirror-like interpenetration of systems

the closer left-hand shore
(the red roofs of Gatow)
was flying backwards
like a violently tugged tablecloth
while the right-hand shore
stayed (apparently) in place

—the overthrow of determinism
marvellous coexistence of possibilities

—my greatness—
Heym was saying to himself
(he was now gliding backwards
with the left leg raised)
is based on the discovery
that in the contemporary world
there are no direct results
no tyranny of sequence
dictatorship of causality
all thoughts
actions
objects
phenomena
lie side by side
like the traces of skates
on a white surface

a weighty assertion
for theoretical physics
a dangerous assertion
for the theory of poetry

2

those who stood on the right shore
didn't notice the disappearance of Heym

the high school student passing him
saw everything in reverse order:

white sweater
trousers fastened below the knee
with two bone buttons

calves in orange stockings
the skates the cause of the accident

two policemen pushed a path
through the crowd of onlookers
standing over the hole in the ice

(it looked like the entrance to a dungeon
like the cold mouth of a mask)

licking their pencils
they tried to record the event
to introduce order
according to the obsolete
logic of Aristotle

with the slow-minded
indifference of authority
for the discoverer
and his thoughts
which were now
wandering helplessly
under the ice

Mr Cogito's Game

1

The favourite amusement
of Mr Cogito
is the game Kropotkin

it has many merits
the game Kropotkin

it liberates the historical imagination
the feeling of solidarity
it is played in the fresh air
it abounds in dramatic episodes
its rules are noble
despotism always loses

on the big board of the imagination
Mr Cogito sets the pieces

the king designates
Peter Kropotkin in the Pietropavlovsk Fortress
the bishops are three soldiers and a sentry
the castle is the carriage of escape

Mr Cogito can choose
among many roles

he can play
beautiful Sophia Nikolaevna
she smuggles the plan of escape
in a watch case

he can also be the violinist
in the grey cottage
especially rented
opposite the prison
who plays the Abduction from the Seraglio
which means the street is clear

most of all however
Mr Cogito likes
the role of Doctor Orestes Weimar

at the dramatic moment
he distracts the soldier
at the gate by talking

—ever see a microbe Vanya
—never seen one
—and the beast is crawling on your skin
—don't say that your honour
—yes it creeps and has a tail
—big?
—three or four versts

then the fur cap
falls on the sheepish eyes

and already
the game Kropotkin
is moving rapidly along

the king-prisoner runs with great bounds
he struggles for a moment with his flannel bathrobe
the violinist in the grey cottage
plays the Abduction from the Seraglio
voices are heard catch him
Doctor Orestes spins on about microbes

beating of the heart
hobnailed boots on the pavement
at last the carriage of escape
the bishops can't move

Mr Cogito
is happy as a child
again he has won the game Kropotkin

2

so many years
for so many years
Mr Cogito plays

but never
was he attracted by the role
of the hero of the escape

not because of dislike
for the blue blood
of the prince of anarchists
nor abhorrence for his theory
of reciprocal aid

nor is it due to cowardice
Sophia Nikolaevna
the violinist in the grey cottage
Doctor Orestes
also risked their heads

with them however
Mr Cogito
identifies himself almost completely

if it was necessary
he would even be the horse
for the carriage of the fugitive

Mr Cogito
would like to be the intermediary of freedom

to hold the rope of escape
to smuggle the secret message
to give the sign

to trust the heart
the pure impulse of sympathy

but he doesn't want to be responsible for what
will be written in the monthly *Freedom*
by bearded men
of faint imagination

he accepts an inferior role
he won't inhabit history

What Mr Cogito Thinks about Hell

The lowest circle of hell. Contrary to prevailing opinion it is
inhabited neither by despots nor matricides, nor even by those
who go after the bodies of others. It is the refuge of artists,
full of mirrors, musical instruments, and pictures. At first
glance this is the most luxurious infernal department, without
tar, fire, or physical tortures.

Throughout the year competitions, festivals, and concerts
are held here. There is no climax in the season. The climax is
permanent and almost absolute. Every few months new trends

come into being and nothing, it appears, is capable of stopping the triumphant march of the avant-garde.

Beelzebub loves art. He boasts that already his choruses, his poets, and his painters are nearly superior to those of heaven. He who has better art has better government—that's clear. Soon they will be able to measure their strength against one another at the Festival of the Two Worlds. And then we will see what remains of Dante, Fra Angelico, and Bach.

Beelzebub supports the arts. He provides his artists with calm, good board, and absolute isolation from hellish life.

Mr Cogito on Magic

1

Mircea Eliade is right
we are—despite everything
an advanced society

magic and gnosis
flourish as never before

artificial paradises
artificial hells
are being sold on the streetcorner

plastic instruments of torture
have been discovered in Amsterdam

a maid from Massachusetts
received a baptism of blood

seventh day catatonics
stand on the runways
the fourth dimension will snatch them away
an ambulance with a hoarse siren

along Telegraph Avenue
shoals of beards swim
in the sweet smell of nirvana

Joe Dove dreamt
he was god
and god was nothingness

he floated down slowly like a feather
from the Eiffel Tower

a teenage philosopher
disciple of de Sade
expertly cuts
the belly of a pregnant woman
and with blood paints on a wall
prophecies of extermination

there are also oriental orgies
forced and somewhat boring

2

fortunes grow out of this
branches of industry
branches of crime

industrious ships sail
to bring new spices

engineers of visual debauchery
toil without rest

62

breathless alchemists of hallucination
produce
new thrills
new colours
new moans

and an art is born
of aggressive epilepsy

in time
the depravers will turn grey
and think of atonement

then new prisons
will arise
new asylums
new cemeteries

but this is still a vision
of a better future

for the time being
magic
flourishes
as never before

Mr Cogito on Upright Attitudes

1

In Utica
the citizens
don't want to defend themselves

in town an epidemic broke out
of the instinct of self-preservation

the temple of freedom
has been changed into a flea market

the senate is deliberating
how not to be a senate

the citizens
don't want to defend themselves
they are attending accelerated courses
on falling to the knees

passively they wait for the enemy
they write obsequious speeches
bury their gold

they sew new flags
innocently white
teach their children to lie

they have opened the gates
through which enters now
a column of sand

aside from that as usual
commerce and copulation

2

Mr Cogito
would like to stand
up to the situation

which means
to look fate
straight in the eyes

like Cato the Younger
see in the *Lives*

however he doesn't have
a sword
nor the opportunity
to send his family overseas

therefore he waits like the others
walks back and forth in a sleepless room

despite the advice of the Stoics
he would like to have a body of diamond
and wings

he looks through the window
as the sun of the Republic
is about to set

little remained for him
in fact only
the choice of position
in which he wants to die

the choice of a gesture
choice of a last word

this is why he doesn't go
to bed
in order to avoid
suffocation in sleep

to the end he would like
to stand up to the situation

fate looks him in the eyes
in the place where there was
his head

Mr Cogito on Virtue

1

It isn't at all strange
she is not the bride
of real men

of generals
secretaries of state
prosecutors

she follows them through the ages
this tearful old maid
in an outmoded hat from the Salvation Army
she reprimands them

she drags out of the junkroom
a portrait of Socrates
a little copper cross
old words

while marvellous life reverberates all around
ruddy as a slaughterhouse at dawn

one could bury her
in a silver casket
of innocent souvenirs

she becomes smaller and smaller
like a hair in the throat
like a buzzing in the ear

2

my God
if she was a little younger
a little prettier

if she kept up with the times
swayed her hips
to the rhythm of popular music

maybe then she would be loved
by real men
generals secretaries prosecutors

if she tried
to look presentable
like Liz Taylor
or the goddess of victory

but the smell of mothballs
comes from her
she compresses her lips
repeats her great no

unbearable in her stubbornness
ridiculous as a scarecrow
as the dream of an anarchist
as the lives of the saints

The Monster of Mr Cogito

Lucky Saint George
from his knight's saddle
could exactly evaluate
the strength and movements
of the enemy

the first principle of strategy
is to assess the opponent

Mr Cogito
is in a worse position

he sits
in the low saddle of a valley
covered with thick fog

through fog you do not see
glittering eyes
an open jaw

through fog you see only
the shimmering of nothingness

the monster of Mr Cogito
doesn't really have measurements

it is spread out like low pressure
hanging over the country

you can't touch it
with a pen
or with a spear

were it not for its suffocating weight
and the death it sends down
one would think
it is an abstraction
of the type *informel*

but it exists
for certain it exists

like carbon monoxide
it enters all the windows
poisons the wells
covers bread with mould

the proof of the existence of the monster
is its victims
it is not direct proof
but sufficient

2

reasonable people say
we can live together
with the monster

we only have to avoid
sudden movements
sudden speech

to breathe lightly
to pretend we are not there

Mr Cogito however
does not want a life of make-believe

he would like to come to grips
with the monster on firm ground

he walks out at dawn
into a sleepy suburb
carefully equipped
with a long sharp object

he calls to the monster
on the empty streets

he offends the monster
he provokes the monster

like a bold skirmisher
of an army that doesn't exist

he calls:
come out contemptible coward

through the fog one sees only
the huge snout of nothingness

perhaps at last it will come
to the uneven battle

it ought to happen
possibly soon

before there will be
a fall from inertia
an ordinary death without glory
suffocation from formlessness

Mr Cogito Seeks Advice

So many books dictionaries
obese encyclopedias
but no one to give advice

they explored the sun
the moon the stars
they lost me

my soul
refuses the consolation
of knowledge

    so it wanders at night
    on the roads of the fathers

    and look
    the small town of Braclaw
    among black sunflowers

    this place which we abandoned
    this place which shouts

    it is the sabbath
    as always on the sabbath
    a new Sky appears

    —I'm looking for you rabbi

    —he isn't here—
    say the Hasidim
    —he is in the world of Sheol

—he had a beautiful death
say the Hasidim
—very beautiful
as if he passed
from one corner
to another corner
all black
he had in his hand
a flaming Torah

—I'm looking for you rabbi

—behind which firmament
did you hide your wise ear

—my heart hurts rabbi
—I have troubles

perhaps rabbi Nachman
could give me advice
but how can I find him
among so many ashes

The Abandoned

I did not catch
the last transport

I stayed behind in a town
which is not a town

it doesn't have morning
or evening newspapers

it doesn't have
prisons
clocks
water

I enjoy
great vacations
outside of time

I go
for long walks
through avenues of burned houses
avenues of sugar
of rice
of broken glass

I could write a treatise
on the transformation of civilization into archaeology

2

there is great silence

the artillery in the suburbs
has choked on its own courage

sometimes
all that can be heard
is the bell of collapsing walls
and the light thunder
of sheet metal dangling in the air

there is great silence
before the night of the predators

at times
an absurd airplane
appears in the sky

it drops leaflets
calling for surrender

I would do it willingly
but there is no one to surrender to

3

I live now
in the best hotel

the dead porter
remains on duty in his room

from a hill of rubble
I enter directly
onto the second floor

to the suite
of the former mistress
of the former chief of police

I sleep on sheets of newspapers
I cover myself with a proclamation
announcing the final victory

in the bar there are still
large amounts of liquid for solitude

bottles with yellow fluid
and a label representing
a young man in a top hat
walking rapidly to the east

I have no resentment against anyone
that I was abandoned

I was short of
time
money
the right hand

on a twisted wire
a light bulb
recalling a skull turned upside down

I wait for the victors

I drink to the fallen
I drink to the deserters

I overcame
bad thoughts

I was abandoned even
by the presentiment of death

The Trial

During his great speech the prosecutor
kept piercing me with his yellow index finger
I'm afraid I didn't appear self-assured
unintentionally I assumed a mask of fear and depravity
like a rat caught in a trap an informer a fratricide
the reporters were dancing a war dance
I slowly burned at a stake of magnesia

all of this took place in a small stifling room
the floor the benches creaked plaster fell from the ceiling
I counted knots in the boards holes in the wall faces
the faces were alike almost identical
assessors judges witnesses for the defence and the prosecution
and also the audience—they belonged to the same organization
I vainly hoped the defender was a man from town
but he too was a member of the union of magicians

in the first row sat an old fat woman
dressed up as my mother with a theatrical gesture
she kept raising a handkerchief to her dirty eyes
but she didn't cry
it must have lasted very long I don't know how long
the old blood of the West was rising in the gowns of the judges

the real trial went on in my cells
they certainly knew the verdict earlier
after a short rebellion they capitulated and slowly started to die
one after the other I looked in amazement
at my wax hands

I didn't speak the last word and yet
for so many months years I was composing the final speech
to God to the court of the world to the conscience
to the dead rather than the living
roused to my feet by the guards
I managed only to twist my head and then
the room burst out in healthy laughter
my adoptive mother laughed also
the gavel banged and this was really the end

I don't know if I was hung or if the punishment
was changed to a life sentence I'm afraid however
neither the one nor the other happened
therefore when I wake I don't open my eyes
I don't move my head my hands tight against the body
I breathe lightly because truly I don't know
how many seconds of air I still have left

The Envoy of Mr Cogito

Go where those others went to the dark boundary
for the golden fleece of nothingness your last prize

go upright among those who are on their knees
among those with their backs turned and those toppled in the
    dust

you were saved not in order to live
you have little time you must give testimony

be courageous when the mind deceives you be courageous
in the final account only this is important

and let your helpless Anger be like the sea
whenever you hear the voice of the insulted and beaten

let your sister Scorn not leave you
for the informers executioners cowards—they will win
they will go to your funeral and with relief will throw a lump of
    earth
the woodborer will write your smoothed-over biography

and do not forgive truly it is not in your power
to forgive in the name of those betrayed at dawn

beware however of unnecessary pride
keep looking at your clown's face in the mirror
repeat: I was called—weren't there better ones than I

beware of dryness of heart love the morning spring
the bird with an unknown name the winter oak

light on a wall the splendour of the sky
they don't need your warm breath
they are there to say: no one will console you

be vigilant—when the light on the mountains gives the sign—
    arise and go
as long as blood turns in the breast your dark star

repeat old incantations of humanity fables and legends
because this is how you will attain the good you will not attain
repeat great words repeat them stubbornly
like those crossing the desert who perished in the sand

and they will reward you with what they have at hand
with the whip of laughter with murder on a garbage heap

go because only in this way will you be admitted to the company
    of cold skulls
to the company of your ancestors: Gilgamesh Hector Roland
the defenders of the kingdom without limit and the city of ashes

Be faithful Go

Notes

page 3 'Island'

The order of the poems is not strictly chronological, although the poems in Part II (1969–1975) were all written after the poems in Part I (1950–1968); 'Island', for example, was published in Herbert's fourth collection of poems (1968), 'Never About You' appeared in his second collection (1957), and 'See' in his first (1956). The order of the poems in the present selection of translations has been established by Mr Herbert.

page 5 'White Stone'

The text for this poem was taken from *Hermes, Pies i Gwiazda* (*Hermes, Dog, and Star*), Herbert's second collection of poems. It was not included in his *Wiersze Zebrane* (*Collected Poems*) of 1971.

page 8 'Classic'

This and the following six poems are all taken from Herbert's second book, in which some sixty prose poems appear together in the second half of the book. These prose poems were originally conceived as a separate volume of *bajeczki* or fairy tales.

page 14 'Hermes, Dog, and Star'

This was the title poem of Herbert's second collection of poems.

page 20 'Shore'

'It' is literally 'she', the Polish word for 'soul' being of feminine gender.

page 20 'Prologue'

This was the first poem in Herbert's fourth collection of poems, entitled *Napis* (*Inscription*), and it introduces the collection as a whole.

'Gryf', 'Wilk', and 'Pocisk' are pseudonyms of partisans, given in Polish. They mean literally 'Griffin', 'Wolf', and 'Bullet'.

page 24 'Warsaw Cemetery'

'an avenue of the living / and the new world' refers to one of the main thoroughfares in Warsaw, which is called the Street of the New World.

page 28 'To the Hungarians'

This poem is from Herbert's second volume of poems, where it has the title '*Stoimy na granicy . . .*' ('*We stand at the border . . .*'). The original title, '*Węgrom*', as well as the date at the end of the poem, were deleted by the censor. We have restored the original title and the date.

81

page 45 'Sequoia'

'Mount Tamalpais' is in Marin County north of San Francisco; the poem was written during a visit to the United States in 1969. The 'unfortunate Harold' was killed by a Norman arrow which struck him in the eye.

page 48 'Damastes (Also known as Procrustes) Speaks'

This poem—as well as 'Anabasis' and 'The Monster of Mr Cogito—has not yet been collected in book form; the translations are based on the versions which appeared in the periodical *Twórczość*, 7, lipiec, 1974.

page 57 'Mr Cogito's Game'

'*Freedom*' is written in English in the original Polish text.

page 67 'Mr Cogito on Virtue'

This poem, as well as 'The Abandoned' and 'The Trial', has not yet been published; the translations are based on the author's typescripts.

page 69 'The Monster of Mr Cogito'

When asked about his use of the French word 'informel', Mr Herbert has said that it refers to a kind of abstract painting without form or outline, in which the composition is open and imprecise.

page 79 'The Envoy of Mr Cogito'

This is the last poem in the collection entitled *Pan Cogito* (*Mr Cogito*), and the imperative which is the first and last word in the poem refers in large part to the book as a whole.